JOURNAL

I Know you are Embarking on
a Wonderful journey full of Mystery
and Surprise, Exciting Days ahead!
There will be Some day's that Seem Better
Then others. Just Remember there all Good!

I can remember Singing to you when you
were still in your Mother's womb and How
you would Squeeze my Pinkie when you
were learning to WALK. I wish I had written
all of it Down. You have grown up So fast
and I am So proud of you. You are the Best
thing that has ever HAppened to my life.

I thought I would
give you this Journal
So you could Document
your Wonderful Journey! Love DAD.

PETER PAUPER PRESS, INC.
WHITE PLAINS, NEW YORK

PETER PAUPER PRESS
Fine Books and Gifts Since 1928

OUR COMPANY

In 1928, at the age of twenty-two, Peter Beilenson began printing books on a small press in the basement of his parents' home in Larchmont, New York. Peter—and later, his wife, Edna—sought to create fine books that sold at "prices even a pauper could afford."

Today, still family owned and operated, Peter Pauper Press continues to honor our founders' legacy—and our customers' expectations—of beauty, quality, and value.

Josephine Wall, whose paintings are well-loved the world over, paints in her cottage studio in Dorset, England. Her passion for nature and myth resonate in her intricately detailed artwork that weaves together the romantic and the surreal, as in this journal cover image, *Heart of the Tree*.

Copyright © 2016
Peter Pauper Press, Inc.
202 Mamaroneck Avenue
White Plains, NY 10601
All rights reserved
ISBN 978-1-4413-2078-0
Printed in China
28 27

Visit us at www.peterpauper.com

September 9, 2023

I wanted to journal things going on in this time.

The last major worldwide problem was covid. Covid (coronavirus disease) actually started in late 2019, but got it's worse in 2020. We had to wear masks and ~~so~~ backbone stores closed. The emotions people had were mixed. Some people were angry, thinking covid was a planned outbreak by the government to try to keep us sedated and scared; however some people thought it was an animal disease (a bat) that devoloped into a virus. At the time, I was in 6th-7th grade when we had to stay in lockdown. The emotional and educational distance I and every student had felt was abudant. People had barely passed classes and their educational persuit lessoned. An everyday, online schedule looked something like this.

7:00 am
log onto an online server and join the online video call with your teacher and other classmates for your first class

11:00 am
a lunch break

3:00
log off your laptop and you'd finish your school day

in 2020, many other things happened

Our country was split into republican and democratic
view points. Being Republican meant you most likely
supported